Denial
Is A
Wonderful Thing

by Christina Augello
& John Caldon

Denial Is A Wonderful Thing

by Christina Augello and John Caldon
Copyright © 2017 by Christina Augello
All rights reserved

Denial Is A Wonderful Thing premiered at Under St. Mark's Theatre in New York City in February 2017 as part of FrigidNYC. It was then performed at EXIT Theatre in San Francisco in June 2017 as part of Talk Story: A Storytellers Festival, at the Imperial Theatre in Saint John New Brunswick Canada in August 2017 as part of the FUNDY Fringe Festival, at The Gotham Storytelling Festival and the United Solo Festival in November 2017 in New York.

written by Christina Augello and John Caldon
performed by Christina Augello
directed by Ryan Marchand
lighting design by Curtis Overacre
sound design by Gregory Scharpen

Published by EXIT PRESS
Book design by Richard Livingston
Cover photo and author photo by Steven Crouch

For performance inquiries, contact mail@theexit.org

For additional information about
EXIT PRESS, go to
www.exitpress.org

Paperback ISBN: 978-1-941704-16-5

EXIT PRESS
156 Eddy Street
San Francisco, CA 94102-2708
mail@theexit.org

First Edition: October 2017

Dedicated to all those who have lived my story with me. Thanks for the memories.

NOTES ON THE PLAY

John Caldon and I began work on *Denial* about 4 years ago. I had done several solo shows based on historical women and each time I was asked about doing a show on my own life. I'm primarily an actor so writing was a new and daunting challenge. But as fate would have it I met John Caldon, an accomplished playwright, and became aware of his approach to personal storytelling. I liked it.

John and I began to meet weekly. I would talk and John would listen and tape my stories. He then transcribed the tapes, which covered my six decades on this planet, that's a lot of stories. "Thank you John." We began to look for the pieces of the puzzle that would make a theatrical picture. We workshopped a couple different approaches until we discovered *Denial* as the thread.

In April 2016 we presented two readings. With the valuable feedback we received we worked together and developed what is now *Denial Is A Wonderful Thing*. It's been an incredible journey to relive my life's ups and downs. I wasn't sure I could do something so personal on stage but when the show was pulled in the FRIGID lottery, a New York Fringe Festival, I figured the universe had made that decision for me. Working with John and Ryan Marchand, my director, Gregory Scharpen, sound designer and Curtis Overacre, light designer has brought it all together in a genre we call Talk Story, a Hawaiian phrase meaning "an informal chat". As an actor who has played many characters on stage, it's an interesting challenge to play myself as character.

— *Christina Augello*

DENIAL IS A WONDERFUL THING

I met him in Mumbai.

I had just sat down at the Leopold Café next to a wall riddled with bullet holes from their recent spree of terrorist attacks. Ever since then, the place has been guarded by skinny, old Indian men in rickety wooden chairs, armed with rifles that looked like they came from our civil war. I saw them and thought to myself: "Are we safer now?"

The café has a door that opens right onto the Colaba District, a big tourist area in Mumbai. People roam the streets selling things all day long. Maimed children beg for loose change.

I was told that their maiming was intentional – a strategy to increase their daily haul – and I wondered how that could be true. But I'd just come from a screening of 'Slumdog Millionaire' at a nearby cinema, and my mind was stuck on that. Slumdog Millionaire was shot in Mumbai, right where I was.

I ordered a beer, which I don't usually drink. A Foster's because that seemed to be what they had. So I'm just sitting there, looking outside, drinking my Foster's.

And there we were, tourists looking like a bunch of millionaires to these so-called slumdogs hanging out in front of the Leopold Café. The scene was mesmerizing.

In India it's outrageously beautiful one moment: bright colors, gorgeous women, incredible silks. Then you turn your head this way, and without even moving your feet, you'll see naked babies in the gutter playing with rats.

India is a place of extremes. Much like myself.

And there they were, dragging their legs along, begging. An old woman begging, who on my way into the café would not let go of my arm. Aggressive beggars and aggressive sellers and all sorts of aggressive things happening right there in front of the Leopold Café.

And there I was, alone, watching it all through the big open roll-up door. I'd come to India on a bit of a lark, always looking for that elusive romantic adventure I've spent a lifetime chasing.

And there he was, pacing back and forth in Mumbai.

He was rabidly smoking a cigarette. His t-shirt said "Hanoi." I'd always wanted to go to Vietnam, but hadn't been yet. "Has he been to Hanoi?" I wondered.

He was dark skinned. Half Scot and half Aborigine, I would later learn. He was attractive. An odd sort of attractive, if you know what I mean.

And in an instant, I was on an adventure. Because for me, men have always been an adventure.

FATHER DURING CHILDHOOD

My father was a huge personality. His favorite saying was: "You don't have to be hungry to eat." He also used to tell me: "You women are lucky. You can have anything you want. You're sitting on a cash register."

To this day I feel a sense of power around that. I'm mean I'm a strong woman and I like being valued for my intelligence and my abilities. But I also like being pretty. I like the attention. There's something powerful in that, too.

My dad ran a place in Buffalo he inherited called Jew Murphy's Omega Café. It was a speakeasy before it became a bar and restaurant. He was also a fence and a bookie out of the place.

Plus, for a while he ran women and numbers out of The Melody Grill, his spot in the Black neighborhood. My dad also worked for the city for – for the garbage department. Never collected garbage a day in his life, but always collected a pay check.

My grandfather was a hitman for the mafia – my father's father. He didn't want my father to grow up in that life, but my Dad was a Sicilian and to him, that was just the way it was.

I remember when he had a heart attack in his late thirties. My brother Michael, who was really tight with him, was only sixteen at the time. My Dad gave him his gun and his Cadillac, and told him to go down to the Melody Grill, to go into the back room, and to collect what was due.

He lived that kind of life. A rich, colorful life, where you'd just take off to Cuba or drive down to Miami. He liked walking on the wild side and he had 'the juice.'

Buffalo in the fifties and sixties was a theater town. It had been since vaudeville. You had road shows coming through all the time.

Dom De Louise got engaged in my father's restaurant. Edgar Bergen and Charlie McCarthy ate there all the time. One morning my Dad brought Colleen Dewhurst home for breakfast while she was playing Josie in "A Moon for the Misbegotten" at the local rep. Hey back in the day Mae West used to drink at the bar. It was that kind of a place.

I got to go to the theater all the time. One night I went to see Arthur Miller's "After the Fall." That night after curtain I got to go backstage and I'll never forget watching the woman who played the Marilyn Monroe part as she pulled off her blonde wig, she was really a brunette.

I was awestruck, star struck: "That wasn't her at all." Who knew denying reality could be so much fun! I liked it.

My father introduced me to theatre. He'd take me to night clubs and floorshows, and have them parade me around onstage. I got to meet the tall beautiful dancers, and the tuxedoed emcees, and one year at Christmas I got to ride in the sleigh on stage for the Holiday show.

My mother was a beautiful woman. Tall and statuesque with flaming red hair. Elegant in her Boucle knit suits and furs. She made me beautiful dresses in velvet and satins. And always told me: "If you act like a lady, people will treat you like a lady."

Because she didn't like the taste of alcohol, she would sit next to my father in the night clubs, nursing a Brandy Alexander.

My dad always gave me money to tip the piano players. I'd walk up proudly with my dollar in my hand, stand on my tippy toes, and drop it into the huge brandy glass.

Then I'd lean in and whisper: "Please play Tenderly." We always asked for 'Tenderly' my dad and I, it was our song.

It's a life I still love, and this thing I love about living. Glittery curtains, theatricality, romance and drama. Players drinking martinis and smoking cigarettes and sitting at the front table because they know the right people. It's what drew me to the stage in the first place.

BACK AT THE LEOPOLD

I was drawn to the odd attractive man in the Hanoi t-shirt, and watched him as he stamped out his cigarette on a pile of rubble pretending to be a sidewalk in Mumbai. He came inside and slid up to a bar across the room from me. Though I was conscious of his presence, I was not flirting.

Then all of a sudden, he was standing next to my table. He leaned in and said: "Do you speak English?" in his thick Aussie accent. I wanted to say: "Do you?" But instead I invited him to sit down.

My adventure was about to begin.

He got on my case for drinking Foster's, which he deemed the worst beer in the world, Australian. We ordered other beers. I let him choose. And then we started talking like nobody's business. It was one of those instantaneous connections, you know? When you just start talking to someone and it feels like there's nobody else in the room.

Today was his fiftieth birthday and I thought, at sixty-two, I wasn't that much older.

Kym, as I learned his name to be, had been trekking around northern India for the past three months. He was heading back to Australia soon so this would be the last leg of his journey.

At the time I imagined him to be this mysterious world-traveler, which didn't turn out to be the case. But in that moment all I thought was, here's this tall, dark attractive man with an Australian accent who's interested in me.

As it grew darker outside and the room began to fill up with people, we decided to retreat to our respective hotels to freshen up and then meet for dinner back here at the Leopold.

Later that night we met upstairs in a secluded corner. We had cocktails and dinner and continued our we've-known-each-other-our-entire-lives conversation. You know, that instant rapport you sometimes have with a person?

It was just (she makes a hand gesture that means "exquisite"), you know what I mean?

And there was this little underlying, I wasn't sure if we were going to be friends, or if a sexual thing was about to happen. It really wasn't clear to me, but it sure was fun.

We were flirtatious without being overly flirtatious. Until at one point, after dinner, as we sat talking and drinking, he leaned in and said: "You know, Christina, you're a very attractive woman."

And I thought: "Ah, here it comes." But I also thought: "I'm not sure." So I simply said: "Thank you."

We went on and on, and realized that we both enjoyed smoking and getting high and he had some hashish.

He was that kind of a guy who would just go across the street in India and cop some hashish without any concern for his own well being, which scared the shit out of me, but was also exciting. Risk taking turns me on.

Kym was staying in a ten-dollar a night hotel close by the Leopold. It was basically a dormitory with small cubicles and walls that didn't reach the ceiling.

There were two guys at the front desk and a shower down the hall. Mostly men stayed there and local travelers. So my going with Kym to his hotel was pretty racy in itself.

We went to his room, smoked hashish and talked, still enjoying that instant rapport. Then he said he wanted to show me the backside of Mumbai so we went out and wandered the dark streets and alleys for hours and hours.

Kids on the street in India are always bumming something, they'd say: "Give me money for diapers for my baby," but Kym instead of giving them money, would go in and buy them diapers, and then come out and start a conversation. He fell right into the local community.

Close to dawn we went back to his room and had sex. Intense sex, passionate sex, fun and loving sex. We were both hungry for it. I hadn't been with anyone for a while and neither had he. We were two starving beings who found each other in Mumbai, attracted like magnets.

After, as he smoked his cigarette, we continued our esoteric conversation about our lives and ourselvs as he gently stroked my back.

Kym's mother was Aborigine. His father was a Scotsman who he'd never met. So Kym grew up with his mother. In Australia they were still taking any European blooded children away from their Aborigine parent because they literally believed them to be animals not capable of raising civilized children.

So Kym's mother fled Adelaide to another part of Australia, so they wouldn't take him from her. She ran away with him so that she could keep him.

DISCOVERING ADOPTION

My father – or the man who I always think of as my father – met my mother when I was two and fell in love with both of us. I was his little princess. He married my mother when I was four and didn't want me to know that he wasn't my dad.

Now, my mother wanted the guy with the pipe and the slippers, but she fell in love with my father. He introduced her to 'the life' and she got on the merry-go-round. My dad always had mistresses and played around. And he loved to gamble with all his money, win or lose.

My mother was always pregnant. I have five younger brothers. There was always one in diapers and one on the way. Abandoned and alone, alcohol became her escape. And she got good at it. She went from being a loving, caring mother to becoming a world class alcoholic.

I think that's when things started to unravel. When she would get completely hammered she would always hurl this one particular phrase at me: "If you only knew, you'd be grateful."

She said that to me repeatedly in her drunkest moments: "If you only knew, you'd be grateful."

Knew what?

In our dining room we had one of those big old buffet cabinets. One day I remember digging in there looking for something. I don't know what propelled me to do that. Probably because she kept saying that to me.

I don't know what I was looking for. Looking for the truth. Looking to solve a mystery. Looking for somebody who cared because it seemed like everyone else was going south on me.

Way back in the buffet behind lots of stuff I found a wedding picture of my mother and my father with me as their flower girl. Maybe I was born out of wedlock. Maybe that was the thing that I didn't know for which I should be grateful.

But then I came across an insurance policy with another man's name on the line where my father's should have been. The insurance certificate listed an Edward Swan as my father. But I had never heard of him, so it had to be a mistake.

I was in such denial and so afraid to put the pieces together that I just shoved it all back into the darkest corner of the buffet.

Then, as my mother's drinking got worse, the drunken stupors came more and more often. We were at odds with each other in so many ways. She was openly jealous of my relationship with my father.

Then things started escalating. At high school there was a girl who was a cousin through marriage into my father's family. I invited her to come to my graduation party.

"It's at my father's restaurant."

To which she replied: "Don't you mean your step father?"

Enough! This has to be dealt with.

And all the while my mother kept slurring: "If you only

knew, you'd be grateful."

Okay, I did know because I had seen that insurance certificate. But I chose to deny it because it was just too heavy.

And yet, I found myself marching up the steps of City Hall, determined to find out, only to discover that there was no record. They'd had it destroyed.

My father was a criminal, and like all criminals, he knew a judge. So, in addition to listing him as my father, my false birth certificate is dated 1951, even though I was born in 1947.

I was trapped in a lie that I loved.

The next time my mother came at me in the middle of the night and said: "If you only knew, you'd be grateful." I simply said: "Then tell me."

That really threw her, but she told me. Mostly, I think she told me to hurt my father, because she knew he didn't want me to know.

And maybe she told me out of a sense of guilt. I mean she must have had a tremendous amount of guilt all those years hiding a secret like that. Or trying to hide a secret, as the case may be.

She asked me if I wanted her to tell my father that I knew. But I was so worried about his feelings, I pleaded with her: "Nooooo."

I never even considered my own feelings. I never even thought about what it did to me.

The day after my mother told me her secret, I came home to find her sitting sober at the kitchen table flanked by my aunt and my grandmother. Sicilian women.

My father had told them I knew about the adoption. He found out during a fight when my mother threw it in his face. All the support I got from them was my grandmother demanding: "Who told you?"

I had to give my mother up, which didn't make me feel very good. And still nobody asked me how I felt about it. Nobody ever asked me how I felt about it.

Around then my father divorced my mother. Or my mother divorced my father. For many reasons. And that was the end of it. Our relationship just seemed to fade away. I mean, I saw him, but his emotional abandonment hurt me deeply.

LAST DAY WITH KYM IN INDIA

I definitely felt ballsy being with Kym at his hotel. Every time I walked in there was a hushed conversation between the men at the desk. They spoke in Hindi, but I'm pretty sure they were calling me a whore.

We would spend hours and hours laying together in his little cubicle. We'd have sex, then head out, bounce around, get more hashish and head back for more sex.

I was scheduled to fly out at two the next morning. He was going to be there another couple days, so I suggested we go back to my hotel where I could take a hot shower and get my stuff packed. We could hang out there and it would be much more comfortable.

It was late in the evening when we went to my hotel just a few blocks away, but the older guy who ran the elevator wouldn't let him in. He just said: "No visitors after a certain hour."

Kym says: "We're just going up to have tea, mate. We're just going up to have tea."

But the old guy just said: "No visitors."

I sometimes think, because Kym was dark skinned, that there was a prejudicial racist thing going on. Plus I was a woman alone in India bringing back a strange man. I'd been there for two weeks and hadn't brought anyone back, and here I was bringing this man back late at night.

But there was no way he was going to let Kym in, so this would be our last moments together in India. There were hugs and kisses and "we'll be in touch."

I knew him for less than forty-eight hours, but it was the most intense less-than-forty-eight-hours that I had ever spent.

STATE HOSPITAL

My parents' relationship was very intense.

Early in their marriage, when their love was still on fire, my father had a portrait painted of my mother. It hung over the fireplace, beautiful and lifelike. The kind where her eyes would follow you. You know, one of those.

Whenever they had a fight, my mother would take the picture down. So you always knew when you came home, if the picture was down, they were having a fight.

The next thing would be my father upstairs in their bedroom packing his clothes to move to the Genesee Hotel. This seemed to happen over and over again in my early high school years.

They never hit each other, but I do remember being woken up in the middle of the night by my mother throwing every dish against the kitchen wall.

One time she locked my father out, but he simply smashed his way in through the front plate glass window.

That's when my mother's drinking got even worse. My brothers and I would wait up for hours and hours for her to come home.

One time, my brother Billy and I waited up until three in the morning. Finally, she came home, stumbled upstairs, and passed out. Twenty minutes later there were cops at the door. Apparently she had side swiped six cars and left hers parked and running in the middle of the street.

Another night I remember waking up to the house filled with smoke. She had passed out with a lit cigarette on the couch and it was smoldering beneath her.

I mean, it was scary. We were living in a war zone.

In a sober moment, my mother asked me what she could do. She was crying like a little girl.

She wanted to not drink. She really wanted to quit drinking and be a good mother.

I told her: "I can't help you. You need to talk to a professional."

Soon after, in one of her drunken stupors, she decided to head to the State Hospital and sign herself in. So, she goes to the hospital grounds and lets herself into some doctor's house where she winds up passed out on his couch.

This poor man comes home to find my drunk mother passed out on his couch.

I became the mother. I was eighteen with five younger brothers, one whom was a baby. My father refused to get her out. Her stepfather, who was kind of around at the time, wouldn't go. So I went to rescue my mother.

I remember sitting in the psychiatrist's office, and he asks me: "Why do you think your mother drinks?" I told him: "You should ask her that. I just want to take her home."

But they wouldn't let me because apparently when you sign yourself into the State Hospital the law says you have to stay for two weeks.

But they did let me see her.

Long hallway.

Black and white tiles.

Horrifying brightness.

And way at the other end, my mother behind bars.

I walk closer and closer and she's sobbing. Finally, from the other side of the bars she looks at me and says: "I suppose you're going to let them keep me here?"

That's when I decided to leave home. Because this was going nowhere fast. And whatever spirit I had in me was disappearing with it.

And all the life I had lived had taught me that there was something more. That there was a rich, colorful adventure waiting for me, and I was going to go out and get it.

CONSTANT CONTACT WITH KYM

Kym and I kept in touch every day with emails and phone calls. Our discovery of each other was phenomenal. We both romanticized to the hilt, being long distance lovers.

He talked about coming here, but then couldn't because of such and such, and such and such, and such and such. He was a dreamer, which is a constant attraction for me.

Then his stories started to wind around to he couldn't come here, but why didn't I come there? Well we had really chucked a lot of shit into less than forty-eight hours. It was intense, revealing, open, like I've known you all my life. Like, where have you been all my life?

Plus I'd never been to Australia and was intrigued by his stories about the outback. About how he grew up and who he was for having lived there.

MICHAEL

When I was living in New York City – after I'd hitchhiked from San Francisco and missed my chance to go to Woodstock back in the summer of '69 – I met the man I was going to marry.

Michael was a drug dealer from Buffalo, and of course, one of those kind of guys. And not just a drug dealer, but the drug dealer. A very handsome, tall, good looking ladies-man kind of guy. My best friend, Suzanne, who I hitchhiked with to San Francisco and back, was good friends with him.

When we got to New York she and I rented a room in one of those residential hotels on the Upper West Side that doesn't exist anymore. You had your little kitchen, with your oven and your burner and a shared bathroom down the hall. That's where we lived.

One night we were talking about the men we had known, as girls do. I told Suzanne that I liked Michael and would love to meet him. She invited him to New York. He stayed with us and romance blossomed.

One night, on the Staten Island Ferry under a full moon, he asked me to marry him. And I said yes.

Boy was that a mistake. Turns out he was already married and had kids, and would have to get a divorce before any of that could happen with us.

But it was romantic and I'm always about the romance and the drama. If it's bigger than life, then it's fun and worth doing.

We stayed in New York and got our own place. Suzanne met someone else. Michael got a job but was still a drug dealer. At some point he went to Buffalo to do some deals.

There he wound up in the hospital with hepatitis. Madly in love, I rushed back to Buffalo to take care of him, to rescue him.

I've rescued a lot of men in my life. My last therapist was very happy when I got my first dog.

We stayed in Buffalo for a while. My dad gave me a job working lunches at Jew Murphy's. When I had called him from New York to tell him I was getting married he was ecstatic but then he met Michael and I don't think a drug dealer was exactly what he had in mind for a son in law.

So I kept thinking if we went somewhere else, a new place that things would be better. I guess that's really what it came down to.

So, we went back to New York and got a place in another residential hotel. Michael got a job working the desk and I was doing office work.

At some point it became clear to me that he was having an affair with a Puerto Rican woman who lived upstairs. So he's married, engaged to me, and having an affair. Which is normal, I guess, for some of the men I've been attracted to.

I remember marching up the stairs and banging on her door, demanding that it be over. I don't know why I was picking on her – I should have been picking on him. I have no idea what she said. She just screamed at me in Spanish.

Michael then started to shoot drugs, which was bad. So I decided if we moved to California things would be better. We would not go to the Haight. We would not go to San Francisco. No, he had a friend who was a musician in Oakland we could stay with.

Now, I don't know why I couldn't put that puzzle together. Why I thought that was going to be any better? But denial is a powerful drug.

We caught a ride with one of those drive away cars, you know, the kind where a person moves across country and you drive their car to them. Michael got a job as a security guard in the City.

And I was working at Mills College for the Dean of

Admissions. And we were going to be married, but then once again, he started having an affair with a rich older woman in the City who had a red MGBGT sports car. Michael always wanted an MGBGT.

So, that was the end of that. I moved out.

I remember calling my mother, who had quit drinking and by then was a pillar in the AA community. She was learning how to nurture people again, but that hadn't quite spilled over to her own kids yet. I called her sobbing: "My life is over." To which she replied: "It will just be easier next time."

By then my friend Suzanne had also moved out to California. I got an apartment in her building upstairs from her. She was helping me mend my broken heart.

Then one morning I looked out the window and saw Michael's car. He wasn't in bed with me. No, he was downstairs in bed with my best friend Suzanne. They later proceeded to get married.

I stood up for their wedding. They invited me to be part of a threesome, which I turned down because that never appealed to me. I'm much too selfish. I just want one-on-one. Pay full attention to me.

And, of course, Michael was happier than a pig in shit. He had two women who adored him. The bastard. He wasn't worth it. Well, maybe in bed he was.

So they got married and had five kids. She just kept having babies. And all I can think is: thank god it wasn't me.

But that's just where we were at. And now I think, what was wrong with that? How did that work? Where did that come from? How did we liberated women fall into that?

I suppose maybe men at that age in my life, and for a long time, held a certain mystique. If I wanted it, I was going to give up whatever I had to give up in order to get it.

GOING DOWN UNDER

So one month later I'm flying into Sydney on my way to Adelaide. I'm all pressed and gussied up for the next part of my adventure.

When I got off the plane, Kym was there waiting for me, smiling. But he looked kind of tired, worn out, hadn't shaved. Not bright and happy with flowers in his hands.

The first thing he says to me is: "I need to tell you right now that my situation has changed. There's some money involved. I have to settle a debt and the only way I can settle this debt is to run some weed from Adelaide up to Alice Springs. I don't want to mess up our visit, but that's just where I'm at. I'm sorry. You can decide if you want to come with me or not."

I just traveled ten thousand miles, and: "He wasn't talking about heroin. He wasn't talking about cocaine." Because that would have scared me. Probably.

But pot? I mean, really? He's going to run a couple pounds of weed from Adelaide up to Alice Springs where he has family and friends, and sell it there, and we'll have fun along the way.

So I thought: "Sure, why not? A little drug run. Ha ha."

STARTING THE AUSTRALIAN ADVENTURE

We went to his place in Adelaide to hang out overnight. In the morning we got into his car and drove for quite a while to his brother's house. His brother had one of those campervans with two sides that open up so you can store stuff and sleep, if you have to.

Now I hadn't slept for probably two days now. Then we started drinking tequila shots and all that kind of stuff.

We're yapping away. People are coming over, making food.

I think we had sex, but I don't really remember because I had taken a valium. Well, I know we had sex because I woke up the next morning with a big hickie on my neck. But I don't remember much.

Finally, after I'd slept some, we got on the road in his brother's car. We brought the pot with us from Adelaide. This lady he knows grows it there.

The first morning after I woke up I was hungry and Kym says we were going to go get some pies. I thought: "Pies, I don't want pie in the morning. I'm hungry. I want breakfast."

But we drove to this place that makes pies – kangaroo pies, ostrich pies, beef pies, all sorts of delicious homemade pies. So we got our pies and hit the road, driving and talking and talking and driving.

HITCHHIKING

Back in 1969 I hitchhiked with my friend Suzanne from Buffalo to San Francisco. We dropped acid at a party one night and decided to head west.

I sold my brass bed for thirty-five dollars. It was a gift from my father and one of my prized possessions but now it was my way out. And besides he'd never notice.

We got rides easily. Back then there were lots of people whose kids were on the road, so you'd get picked up by couples who would give you money and feed you, thinking: "My kid's out there somewhere. I hope someone's taking care of them this way" It was a very benevolent time.

Plus, I was traveling with another woman, so there were two of us. So we weren't threatened or scared. I wasn't scared. I've never really been scared. Well, some things scare me. Rats scare me. But adventure doesn't scare me. Go out in the world and see what happens.

When we got to San Francisco, we copped some lime green acid at the corner of Market and Powell next to a huge pit in the ground. They were building BART, San Francisco's underground.

Then we rode the 7-Haight all the way up to Hippy Hill, where we met some people we knew from Buffalo. There were so many people running drugs back and forth back then you always knew somebody.

They took us up to Saint Mary's on California and Grant where you could get a ticket for a hotel room. If you were a woman, you couldn't get it alone. But if you had a guy with you, they'd give you one.

So we got a ticket for a hotel somewhere down on Sixth Street below Mission. I hated it because we were tripping on acid and I knew how dirty it was.

You could also get sandwiches from the nuns at Saints Peter and Paul at four o'clock and you could get breakfast at Saint Anthony's. If you were a woman you got to go in first, so there was always some guy hitting on you so he could walk in with you.

Once we found an old suitcase and umbrella. We took it to a pawn shop, then went to a Chinese restaurant where we had enough money to buy a meal from soup to nuts.

That was an adventure. It was exciting. I wasn't down and out. I knew I could go get a job and live differently, if I chose to. But this was cool and it was working.

Then we went to Haight Street. Now that was a little dicey because were two young women and Haight Street in the Summer of '69 had turned from the nice, wonderful, la-la-la drugs to heavy duty downers, junk and speed. It was a nasty place. People didn't go out after dark.

The drugs had become the bad drugs. There are good drugs and there are bad drugs. There are still good drugs and bad drugs, as far as I'm concerned. It had gone to bad drugs.

But it wasn't what I expected the Haight to be. I was a flower child. I wanted to come to the '67 Haight-Ashbury. Or '66, really. Before it ever got to be public, that would have been the best time.

Before is always the best time. Before anyone knows about it. You have to be ahead of the curve to really enjoy it.

Suzanne and I met some drug dealers from Alabama and moved in with them on Haight Street. We'd clean their house and do this and that, so they took care of us. And, of course, we slept with them.

But they were doing drugs all the time. They were shooting acid and had bubbles on their hands, big abscesses. People were just tipping over. They were out of control.

So I decided we had to get out of there. The guy I was with and the guy Suzanne was with would go to the Fillmore at night to sell drugs. We stayed home. By then things had gone south with the relationships.

That night when my lover-guy came back I heard him say where he hid his money. So I decided to take some. We did all the cooking and cleaning so I figured we'd earned it. When he went to sleep, I took half his money.

I remember crawling over and shaking Suzanne quietly awake. We snuck out, went down to Haight and Masonic, got on a bus that took us all the way to Berkeley, so we wouldn't get caught. There we hitched a ride and headed back to New York City.

There were all sorts of escapades on our way back to New York. Once I had to sleep outside in the rain because I didn't want to fuck this guy. Suzanne met someone she liked, but I didn't want to be with the other guy, so they threw me out.

I wound up sleeping under the stairs waiting for her to get done with herself. In the morning she ran out. They threw her out without her shoes. So we ended up hitchhiking all the way back to New York City and she had no shoes.

It was the summer of Woodstock. We caught a ride with a guy who said: "Ladies, would you like to go to Woodstock?" Now she had no shoes and I had just enough money for a phone call.

I told her: "I don't think we should do that. I think we should go to New York City call my friend and get rescued "

So I missed Woodstock. Who knows what would have happened if I had gone to Woodstock.

COPPERS ON THE ROAD

Kym was happy we had his brother's car. Not just because we were camping out or because it would be more comfortable, but because he had made this run one too many times, which he was just now telling me.

So then this happy-go-lucky little drug run became: "You're so concerned people are looking for you that you didn't want to bring your car?"

I had no desire to put that puzzle together. It was just like: "Hmmmm, okay. I can live with that. That's alright. I can do that. That's fine. Everythings's gonna be fine." Denial. Oh, Denial. Eh, Denial. Everythings gonna be fine. I'm on an adventure."

So, Kym and I are driving down the Australian highway — and I'll never forget this — when over the campervan's CB radio some guy says: "Look out. There's coppers on the road."

I'm riding along next to Kym thinking: "Coppers on the road? Who are the goddamn coppers?" That doesn't sound good.

Kym screeched to a halt and said: "There's cops up ahead.

I'm going to hide the pot." Now, we have these two big garbage bags full of pot. He gets out of the car, runs into the woods to stash it, and then we drive off.

I'll never forget the word coppers because it was like: "What kind of adventure am I in? Are we back in the seventies or something?"

DRUG BUST

In 1971 I got busted. For pot. I was charged with two felonies. My grandmother saw me on TV. The reason I was on TV was King. King was a German Shepard. The first dog in Buffalo trained to sniff out pot.

I'd been in Europe for several months hitchhiking around and had come back to Buffalo on my way to California to go to my brother Michael's engagement party and visit old friends.

I had two ounces of pot on me, travelers checks, passport, everything. It was just for me, but in Buffalo that made me a drug dealer. Now I had lived in California for a while, so the uptightness was beyond me.

So there we were, three ladies drinking tea. One of the lady's boyfriends had sent her two pounds of pot railway express so we knew it was coming. The cops came to the door. We didn't know they were cops because they were dressed like railway express.

We signed the paper, brought in the box and set it on the table. We didn't even open it. We knew what was in it. Pot for her to sell.

The doorbell rings again. Same men, but this time they said: "You forgot your receipt." So they give us the receipt and go away.

The third time they came back they pushed their way in,

came barreling down the hallway, tore open the package, held it high in the air and exclaimed: "Aha! Cannabis!"

The whole nine yards. King had sniffed it out. This was King's first bust. Now I had these two ounces of pot in my purse, so when I heard them I opened the side door that goes down to the basement from the kitchen and threw it down there thinking: "Okay. I'm cool."

The cop that busted us had gone to school with my dad. He recognized my name, which had some weight. I thought: "Maybe this will keep me from going to the police station. The box wasn't addressed to me. I'm just sitting here having a cup of tea for god's sake!"

So the officer calls my dad and they decide they're going to straighten everything out down at the station. And I think: "Now I'm really fucked."

Then the cat runs to the basement. So thinking I'm really slick I say to the cop: "You can't leave the poor cat down there. It'll starve to death if you're going to take us all to jail." He let me go.

I don't know what I was thinking, but I went down and grabbed the purse, shoved my I.D., travelers checks, everything down my pants. Then I threw the purse. Threw the pot. Threw everything. And, of course, the cop's standing right there behind me, watching me do it.

I had no idea what I was doing, but I had been raised with criminals, so I thought I could get away with it. But I've learned in my life that you're never smarter than cops or criminals because that's what they do that for a living – you don't.

They take us to the police station. Fingerprint us. Mug shots. My friend's crying: "I don't want to go to prison!"

And the other one's screaming: "They threw the Christians to the lions, too!"

In Buffalo back then the cops and criminals were practically the same people. I remember my father walking in shaking his head. He wasn't into drugs, but that was okay. His whole problem was that I gotten caught.

And my mother who is now a reformed alcoholic and AA up the gazoo, thinks I've been taken over by the devil.

I spent the night in jail. I later learnbed that my mother could have gotten me out, rescued me. One of her AA buddies was a judge who could have signed the paper, but she wanted me to learn a lesson.

The whole thing boiled down to deferred sentencing for six months with a recommendation to drop charges. That meant if I didn't get caught again, it would be wiped off my record.

So I spent all the money I had on a lawyer and hitchhiked back to California, just happy to leave Buffalo.

BACK TO THE COPPERS

So there we were in the middle of Australia hiding pot in the woods. Kym pulls over to the side of the road and says: "We're going to sleep on the ground tonight."

Now, before coming to Australia I had read that there are something like sixteen poisonous snakes in the world and each of those species live in Australia. Or something like that. I don't really remember. But bottom line – there's a lot of snakes and I'm a city girl to begin with.

So Kym says: "We're going to sleep on the ground tonight." And I say: "No we're not." And he says: "It's the winter– no snakes." I say: "Not going to happen."

Begrudgingly he hauled out all of the shit out from inside the campervan so we could sleep in the car. And it just to be like: "Uhhhhh, Uhhh…" You know?

I mean we did a lot of fun things. We were going to the Northwest Territories, which is not a state of Australia. It's the center of Australia, the Outback.

I got to go the camel races and we went to Ayers Rock, which is this huge rock sacred to the Aborigines. Australians, and Aborigine people in particular, don't climb that rock. You're not supposed to. It's just not cool. We drove around it. But you see these big chains and tourists dragging themselves up the side of Ayers Rock. So the old Australia – the Aborigine culture, which is Australia's beginning – was totally disrespected.

And along the way we would check into these different campsites to make deals. But, of course, none of his connections showed up or had the money.

Kym's pot dealing became the paramount issue and I was no longer the paramount issue.

Then the sex started slowing down because the whole focus had changed. We were still having fun, but I thought: "Okay, this is not going to be about me. I'm pretty much just along for the ride."

Finally we arrived in Alice Springs and Alice Springs is pretty cool. It really is the outback. It's very rural, but very hip. It's very hippy, kind of.

For me it was completely retro. It was like the Haight from before. And yet at the same time, I had to remind myself so are the rules, so are the laws, so is everything.

Finally we finished our pot run and we were taking the long way home. We went to Moree, where he grew up. It was really remote. The place from which he'd returned after his mother had run away.

EDWARD SWAN

My mom was raised in and out of foster care. She was an orphan. A Hollywoodesque orphan. Her mother ran off with a traveling salesman. So her father gave her and her twin sister, who were just babies, up for adoption to a rich couple he knew.

But the rich mom dies. So, the rich dad gives them back. Then she goes from one horrible situation to another.

She's adopted by a couple, who really only want her twin sister. When she's a bad girl, she's put in a basket in a dark basement and hoisted up with rope. At sixteen she runs away from home and goes to work in a honky-tonk. There she gets raped.

Then she goes to jail but won't tell them she's under eighteen because she doesn't want to go back home. An older woman in jail counsels her for a month, then tells the authorities she's underage and back home she goes.

As an adult my mother eventually found her birth father, but for her it was a horror story. A dirt poor farmer with a family who needed her more than she needed them. There was no real connection there, but my mom felt obligated to to help, which was a drain on her.

So when I finally decided I could no longer live in denial and told my mother I wanted to find my birth father. She didn't want me to and she refused to help. She told me not to insert myself where I wasn't supposed to be.

At this point I was twenty-six and living with my lover, Richard, who has become my best friend for over forty years. His support gave me the courage I needed to find Edward Swan.

I got as much information from my godmother as I could. She had known Edward and told me he had lived in Arizona before moving to Southern California.

Foolishly I went to the library to look for "Swan" in the phone books. I started with A – Anaheim. Then I worked my way to B – Bakersfield. Finally I said to myself: "This is ridiculous. I'm never going to find him this way."

When I was still with Michael and we were talking about moving to California we had thought about Chula Vista as a place to settle down. So on a whim, I pulled out the Chula Vista phone book and there he was: Edward Swan. I wrote his phone number down, put it in my pocket and went home.

After five days of walking around with the number in my pocket, Richard said: "Either call the number or throw it away. It's one or the other." So on a Sunday morning I dialed the number.

"Hi. My name is Christina and I'm looking for Edward Swan."

"This is Edward Swan. How can I help you?"

I had hoped that after twenty-five years by just saying my name he would know what I was talking about.

"I think you're my father." He started laughing, you know that nervous kind of laugh? "Babe, let me sit down for a second."

We talked for a while. He bought me a ticket to fly down to meet him. But the irony of all this was he was a right-wing, flag carrying ex-cop, who had previously been with the DEA in Arizona.

The first photo he sent me was of him with a rifle, a flag and two dead pheasants. And here I am, a moon-child with long hair, no bra, feather earrings and a see-through top.

When we did meet, Richard went with me. At the time he was interested in buying a women's volleyball franchise in San Diego. What can I say, it was the seventies. We flew down together and got a room at the Blue Belle Motel.

Edward Swan immediately disapproved of that – that I was staying in a room with a man who I wasn't married to. I mean, this guy doesn't even know me and he's already telling me what I'm supposed to do.

We had a nice time. He showed me pictures of myself when I was a baby, which I'd never seen before. My dad used to put me in beauty contests, so I saw a lot of pictures of myself at four, five and six, but never one as a baby.

Edward and I talked a lot and agreed it was probably better that we didn't live close together because we had so many differences, but that it was still really great we'd met each other.

I wish I could say it was one of those stories where I could say he was a millionaire or a Hollywood producer." But that was not to be. You roll the dice. Sometimes you win and other times you get a DEA agent.

GAMBLING

All over Australia you can gamble. Kym and I went to Coober Pedy, an opal mining town where it's so hot they built everything underground. When you go there you just keep going down and down and down.

There's casinos and restaurants, hotels and stores. Kym won six-hundred dollars. He was a gambler. I hadn't realized it, but there was that, too.

He bought me an opal ring and said: "Before I spend all this money I'm going to buy you something nice."

The next night we went to another one of those places. We had something to eat in the restaurant and then went to the gambling room where he won another eight-hundred dollars.

He had been drinking a lot. We all had been drinking a lot.

When Kym went to collect his winnings the blonde, white, Aryan, poster-boy clerk wouldn't pay him right away.

The chips on Kym's shoulder, all that resentment, started coming up. He was half Scot and half Aborigine, but had grown up in a culture that totally disrespects Aborigine blood. And the racism was palpable.

When the clerk refused to pay him right away, he went off on this angry tangent. It was a scary confrontation.

When we got back to the room he kept going and it scared me. I started crying and told him: "I don't like this energy. I don't like what's happening here."

He went into the bathroom, took a shower, came out with a towel wrapped around his waist, and went out the front door. I was happy to see him leave.

In the morning I went outside to see if he was still there and found he had taken the mattress out of the campervan and slept on the ground. He got up, got dressed and we never talked about it.

AN EDWARD SWAN SONG

Edward Swan and I never talked much. The relationship was there but there was no nurturing to it. For a while he kept it up and would send me Harry and David apples and pears at Christmas.

Neither of us really had a reason to keep up the relationship. We both had lives of our own. He died a few years ago. But before, he called to tell me he had some things he wanted to send me.

I received a package from him containing a little department store box from Buffalo. The cotton was yellowed, the box broken.

Inside was the baby bracelet they gave me at the hospital, a tiny ring, a locket, and my baptismal certificate. I was baptized an evangelical Christian, if you can imagine that.

All those years he had saved it all. That was my legacy, I guess.

He wasn't a very adventurous person. Plus he was a cop. Whereas my father who raised me, he and I were simpatico.

For all his tremendous flaws, I loved how he saw life. And I've always kept that with me. And I've always thought, my god how lucky I was that he loved me and raised me.

THE MOON

The sun was setting as Kym and I pulled up to the Oodnadatta Track in the Outback with just enough light to read the warning signs: "Remote Areas Ahead." Followed by a list of precautions.

Precaution one: 'Carry adequate fuel, water, food, current road maps, two spare tires, two jacks, a shovel, first aid kit and tow rope.'

We have none of these.

Precaution two: 'Drink water at regular intervals to avoid dehydration.'

We should have gotten some.

Precaution three: 'Avoid night driving as wild life and livestock may be active.'

Night is upon us.

Precaution four: 'Keep friends or relatives informed of your outback travel itinerary.'

Nobody knows where I am.

And last, in big bold capital letters: 'In the event of a

breakdown, never leave your vehicle.'

I promise myself I won't leave the truck and off we go down the dusty red road. No one to be seen. No cars in front or behind. The blackness descends and the stars appear.

Kym stops, jumps out and waves for me to follow.

"Never leave your vehicle," I think, but he beckons again, and I want to see.

The truck is high and it's a long way down. I step outside and I'm on the face of the moon, the Southern Cross looming large in the blue, black sky.

So alien it terrifies me. A vast darkness, a sea of nothing, much like being alone on stage and not knowing your lines.

Mind blank.

Heart racing.

Fright.

Flight.

Fear sends me running back to the truck.

Inside the truck is my snow globe. I long to be outside, to become part of that Southern Cross. But I'm swallowed up in the globe's murky liquids.

Black.

Silver.

Midnight blue.

I grasp at memories, frightened by their lack of definition, but I'm lured back in by my active imagination.

On the face of the moon.

Or an empty stage.

Or a Buffalo bar.

A figure in a globe. Stuck inside. If only I could see it from the outside. But there is no outside. Just me, a piece in a puzzle seeking a picture. But adventure is creating the picture, not collecting its pieces.

Back in the truck Kym drives us away, leaving that moment behind us, but forever imprinted on me. Kym is a piece in my puzzle, but not the picture. I strain to see that.

RECONNECTING

My relationship with my mom was strained for years. I remember asking her why she stopped drinking and she said – and this really pushed my buttons, totally wiped me out –she said: "I quit drinking because you abandoned me."

"I abandoned you? What the fuck! You abandoned me."

I was hurt. I was devastated when she said that. And probably there was some guilt for having left. I was so upset I started crying and had to leave the house.

It took me years to reconnect with my mom. Then after some therapy, I realized I needed her. I wanted a mom. I needed a mom. And goddammit, she was it.

By then she had become a woman to be reckoned with. Sober, she got an education, and became a mentor and advocate for women like herself. She built safe houses for them, defied the law on their behalf. She realized her dream and her picture. She was a mother to be proud of.

When I reached out to her she said: "I thought you'd never call."

"What? You were going to let your only daughter disappear? Not even reach out?"

She said: "I thought I'd be rejected."

So my mom and I started talking and that talking brought my father back into the mix because those two people still loved each other. They were still connected to each other through five sons and me.

Up to the end she loved him. Their other spouses afterward were always jealous.

She once said: "If I'd stayed with your dad I'd never have become the woman I became. But I never stopped loving him."

When my father re-married, he married his mistress. My grandmother used to say: "That's when he up and married the Pollock." That's what she called her – the Pollock.

My grandmother and my Aunt Josephine actually sat in the car outside the church during his wedding, but wouldn't go in. They just sat there to be annoying. Sicilian women.

DENIAL IS A WONDERFUL THING

My father continued his dalliances into his old age. He was always a flirt. I'm a flirt. He taught me how. I love flirting. There's power in that.

My dad was the guy sitting at the end of the bar, drinking Scotch over, cigarette in hand, diamond pinky ring, flirting with the waitresses.

His second wife was a bit domineering. I don't think he was happy with the Pollock. My cousin Rosalie told me my father once said leaving my mom and marrying that woman was the stupidest thing he had ever done.

I visited my parents in south Florida for Thanksgiving one year. My dad said to me: "Your mom tells me you're uptight because we never told you about…" He trailed off. Didn't finish the sentence.

I guess that was his way of trying to make it better. But you know, I couldn't finish the sentence either. We just looked at each other.

That's the only time I ever remember talking about it. And I believe that neither of us wanted to say it out loud because that would mean what we were wasn't real.

Things are what you think they are until you give up on the thought. Denial is a wonderful thing.

LOST SOUL

Kym and I made our way back to Adelaide and hung out for a couple more days, but it had lost its charm. Being with him in India and the fun of the drug run in the beginning was fantastic, but as things progressed…

My last night there we were making dinner and out of nowhere he had to go somewhere to do something. It took hours for him to come back.

While he was gone, I talked with his roommate, who was incredulous I had come all this way to see him.

He told me: "Kym is a lost soul."

We had a good time, but it was mostly two days of me waiting to leave and questioning why I'd come.

As I sat on the plane watching the passengers board, I tried to put the puzzle together. But the pieces rearranged themselves endlessly. A kaleidoscope of colors and memories.

Then slowly, the pieces fell away, and a picture emerged.

A picture of a woman on a plane by herself, but not alone.

A picture of an incomplete person, who is entirely whole.

A picture of me.

Curtain

ABOUT THE AUTHORS

Christina Augello has been performing since grade school. Her favorite roles are complicated, independent women who make their own choices, good or bad! Some of these include the Baroness Elsa von Freitag-Loringhoven, the Mama of Dada, in *Last Of The Red Hot Dadas*, the grifter turned social worker Bertha in *Boxcar Bertha*, Grace O'Malley, the Irish Pirate Queen in *A Most Notorious Woman*, the courageous and outrageous actress Betty Hutton in *Rat Girl*, the salty Regina Fredrickson in *Confessions Of A Catholic Child* and most recently Elizabeth I in Clive Barker's *Paradise Street* where one critic compared her performance to that of Judy Dench, Bettie Davis and Flora Robson. In *Denial Is A Wonderful Thing* Christina presents the most complicated woman she knows – herself! Christina is also the founder and artistic director of EXIT Theatre and the San Francisco Fringe Festival.

John Caldon is a San Francisco based playwright and director. His work has been seen in the National Queer Arts Festival and the New York International Fringe Festival, as well as at The EXIT Theatre, Bindlestiff Studio, The SF Playhouse, The Thick House, Mama Calizo's Voice Factory, Albuquerque's The Box, the Manhattan Theatre Source and Boston's The Theatre Offensive. He is a graduate of San Francisco State University's Creative Writing program and the Professional Program in Screenwriting at UCLA. His upcoming play *#femmemasculine* will premiere at Brava Theater Center in fall 2017.